NEW-DIMENSIONAL THOUGHT TECHNOLOGY

The Dawning of a New Civilization

ROSSCO

BALBOA.
PRESS

A DIVISION OF HAY HOUSE

Balboa Press books may be ordered through booksellers or by contacting:

Balboa Press
A Division of Hay House
1663 Liberty Drive
Bloomington, IN 47403
www.balboapress.com
1 (877) 407-4847

Because of the dynamic nature of the Internet, any web addresses or
links contained in this book may have changed since publication and
may no longer be valid. The views expressed in this work are solely those
of the author and do not necessarily reflect the views of the publisher,
and the publisher hereby disclaims any responsibility for them.

The author of this book does not dispense medical advice or prescribe the use
of any technique as a form of treatment for physical, emotional, or medical
problems without the advice of a physician, either directly or indirectly. The
intent of the author is only to offer information of a general nature to help
you in your quest for emotional and spiritual well-being. In the event you use
any of the information in this book for yourself, which is your constitutional
right, the author and the publisher assume no responsibility for your actions.

Any people depicted in stock imagery provided by Thinkstock are models,
and such images are being used for illustrative purposes only.
Certain stock imagery © Thinkstock.

Print information available on the last page.

ISBN: 978-1-5043-6561-1 (sc)
ISBN: 978-1-5043-6563-5 (hc)
ISBN: 978-1-5043-6562-8 (e)

Library of Congress Control Number: 2016914472

Balboa Press rev. date: 04/24/2017

I dedicate this book to all the courageous people who together are leading the way to a new civilization.

Contents

P r o l o g u e

Just how long have we waited for this moment?

Between labored breaths,
a young boy wandering the precipice of life and death
caught a fragment of dream flashing before him—
himself, but not himself, straddling the eras.

Magnificent histories and unknown worlds,
gigantic rivers surging from the past and the future,
collide within the young boy.

Now is the time to awaken.

Human suffering will end,
and humankind will be transformed.
I will find the answer.

Introduction

What is the New-Dimensional Thought Technology that the title of this book refers to? It is the answer for humanity—the answer that we humans have ceaselessly sought since the dawn of history.

Humans have a constant desire to know something or reach somewhere, whether we are aware of it or not. But has anyone ever truly achieved this? I think not. We live in a system in which we cannot obtain what we truly desire. Why do we seem to face one problem after another? Why, despite trying so hard to get what we want and be happy, do we fail to do so? Why, once we think we have it, does it suddenly slip through our fingers?

Why? Because this is what we as humans are. During our lifetimes, we go through various experiences, come to know the ups and downs of life, and feel joy and suffering. And such experiences themselves have meaning. Until now, there has been no need to perfect our lives while we are still alive.

The answer, therefore, has been hidden from us. This is why so many people have been absorbed in trying to find themselves, in asking, "Who am I?" But could the self you have found through such haphazard methods be the real you?

Your true self cannot be found, no matter how hard you try, unless you know its origin. Neither will you be able to find the answer. That is because you do not know what the problem is. In this book, I will present a system that makes it possible to fundamentally alter human living, thereby revealing the origin of the true self and the essence of the problem.

When faced with certain vicissitudes of life, such as illness, bankruptcy, or loss, we learn what family love is or discover what is truly important to us. When we do so, our lives often change. In essence, we are able to sublimate these experiences. But what I'm discussing is not just about aiming for a better life or philosophizing about life. It's about making a transformational change that is akin to being reborn within our own lifetimes.

Advances in science and technology have helped make great progress in our lives, such as making our day-to-day existence convenient and comfortable. But what is really happening? Each day, the news is more shocking and so disturbing that we feel there is something seriously wrong, or even dangerous, with the world. Still, we don't know what to do, and we can only hope that these events will not affect us.

But aren't we already affected? We are full of anxiety because we don't know what is going to happen to us, neither where nor when. The future we see at the end of these events is disquieting, to say the least. We carry this anxiety deep within ourselves, but instead of trying to address it, we try to fulfill our material needs and seek comfortable lives. Thus, we run around in total confusion.

The world is always full of contradictions. The Internet has become an indispensable tool in our daily lives, but at the same time, it has become a hotbed of vice and crime. As soon as a new drug is developed to cure a disease, a drug-resistant pathogen evolves. Although we wish to freely enjoy and benefit from scientific and technological progress, it seems that simultaneously, the dark aspects of ourselves that have been suppressed are just waiting for the chance to erupt.

How can we escape from this world of contradictions? We have reached a critical juncture in the way we live as human beings, and continuing to live this way no longer has meaning. We are at the end of the conventional human program—of what I will describe in this book as third-dimensional living.

I have therefore developed a new system of human "software" that can be used by anyone to dismantle the conventional way of living and transcend the human program. The principal purpose in using this system is to initialize and regenerate humans.

For many, words such as *initialization* and *regeneration* may evoke concepts related to the discovery of induced pluripotent stem cells (iPSCs), a scientific breakthrough that has revolutionized the study of cytology. The discovery that cells can be returned to their initial state, enabling internal organs to be regenerated even after losing normal functioning, is immeasurably good news for those who are sick, their families, and even those who are healthy.

With this in mind, what if we could initialize our lives? This is not simply about making our lives better or just starting over. It is about being able to live as if we could accomplish what would otherwise have been left to do in any possible future lives with all the data—our memories—intact.

I have made this possible through my discovery of a system and its practical application, which I call Miross. Through Miross, a human can go back to the life source and consciously reformulate a new life by performing a complete reset. This allows both adults, who have already experienced life's twists and turns, and especially children, whose lives are still uncomplicated, to directly awaken their individual abilities.

What would happen if the laws of the third-dimensional world, with its many limitations, were removed? Through the understanding and practice of this system, a growing number of people have not only instantly solved all sorts of problems related to marriage, family, work, money, and health, but have also started living as if they had been reborn, walking on a completely new path. You will read many of their stories later in this text. This demonstrates the fact that the human race has indeed found a new path on which it is possible to make a completely new step forward.

As you proceed to read this book, the life that you have led will become clearer to you, as will questions about the world and any other thoughts that have floated vaguely through your mind. I can only hope that this book will serve as a summation of your third-dimensional existence and a stepping stone toward transforming your life.

A radical turnaround awaits humanity.

It begins by grasping the greatest deception the
world has played on us: the trap of reversal.

The world we see before us is all reversed.

Thus, not a single thing we have seen is true.

If our lives have not gone well, that is only natural.

Even if life has been going well, everything gets turned
around, and inevitably, we are unable to live the way we want.

But we needn't remain stuck in the world of reversal.
Once we recognize this, we can escape it.

The system of Dual-Structured Coexistence has made
possible what had been thought impossible:
the radical turnaround of humanity.

With this system, we can return what has been reversed,
thus creating High-Dimensional Space
by Reversal with Anti-vector.

For the first time, we can experience our
true selves and live the way we wish
with the world restored to its true state.

Chapter 1

THE ROOT OF ALL PHENOMENA

Everything in This World Is Divided in Two: The Trap of Opposite Polarities

In order to escape from a world bound by the laws of the third-dimensional domain, it is imperative for us to first understand the trap of two opposing polarities that rules this world. Things that we see as opposites, at two extremes, are in fact the same and exist as a pair.

What does it mean to end the conventional human program that I described in the introduction? I should begin by explaining that because of this program, we humans are caught up in a great trap. It is precisely by virtue of this trap that we were able—and compelled—to remain in the third-dimensional domain and experience being human; this very fact, in turn, shows us just how powerful this trap is.

What do I mean by this? To answer, I will begin to dismantle the world we live in, using the Miross system. Let me start by discussing the essence of matter.

Everything in this world exists by virtue of being divided in two. These two polarities are conventionally perceived as opposites; however, they actually exist together as a pair. You may already have a rough idea that everything is divided into two entities that exist as opposite polarities.

For example, once we are aware of life, the opposite notion of death arises. The concept of freedom exists because of its opposite, oppression. It is the same with concepts such as front and back or win and lose. Once we establish the notion of one extreme, the other emerges. Without one polarity, the other cannot exist.

Above all, humans exist as two polarities: man and woman. Even transgender people who have transitioned from one sex to another are by origin male or female, as their chromosomes remain unchanged.[1]

Why is everything in the third-dimensional world where humans live divided in two? In my understanding, it is to put

---

[1] The terms *man* and *woman* and *male* and *female* are used throughout this text; however, it should be noted that Miross is for everyone; it does not exclude people of any sexual orientation. Miross is about a person's inner male and female and the energetics between them. Even if you are homosexual, transgender, or bisexual, you are made of two opposite polarities—that is, two sexes called *maleness* and *femaleness* that exist in you. This is because everyone is born to a father and a mother and inherits twenty-three chromosomes from each one. The union of these two energies, specifically maleness and femaleness, is the essence of Miross.

the human program into operation, to create everything in this world, as well as to know what constitutes this world.

Unless there is a person looking and another being looked at, the act of looking cannot materialize. Thus, it is necessary to have such divisions—the subject doing the looking and the object being looked at. It is my belief that these divisions exist in order to be reunited—that we are in the process of transforming into a new civilization where humanity will live with new consciousness as the old human program ends.

The system of opposite polarities is the basis of all phenomena in our lives. But because everything is divided into two polarities, the world we live in has become a world of optical illusion. We have therefore gone on living and seeking the truth without realizing that we are caught in a trap. I call this conventional way of thinking (where everything is divided in two) third-dimensional thought. The essence of third-dimensional thought is that you and I are different. "Of course we are," you may say. But if you look at it from a new viewpoint—a dimensionally displaced viewpoint—the truth is that you and I are the same.

In looking at two opposite polarities, we encounter a major blind spot, one so obvious that we miss it entirely. The two opposite polarities are actually a pair. The mistake we make is to treat these opposite polarities as separate and opposing entities that engage in a battle against the opposite polarity.

To demonstrate that everything is made up of a pair, let me give you an example that is close to all of us. We were born into this world through our parents. Even if we dislike our parents, disavow any influence from them, or have no memory of them, we cannot deny the fact that we are all born of our parents. In a world where nothing is really 100 percent, this fact alone is 100 percent true.

In addition, we inherited half of our genes, the plus and the minus, from each of these two opposite polarities: a mother and a father. That is the fundamental basis for humans. Unless these two opposite polarities are united, "I" cannot exist (see figure 1).

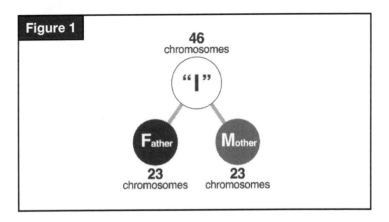

Figure 1

46 chromosomes

" I "

Father

Mother

23 chromosomes

23 chromosomes

So what are the plus and the minus? The two opposites are in fact a pair—different, but a pair. They complement each other and exist simultaneously.

Please refer to figure 2. There are elements of maleness and femaleness inside a man, and likewise, maleness and femaleness inside a woman. These opposite polarities are the same in nature.

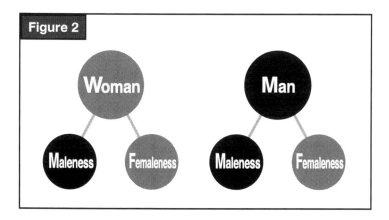

Consider the example of a bar magnet. A bar magnet has two poles, north and south. If you divide it in two by cutting it across the center, the half taken from the north side will have north and south poles, as will the half taken from the south side. In other words, the two halves have the same qualities, even though on the surface, they are opposites (see figure 3).

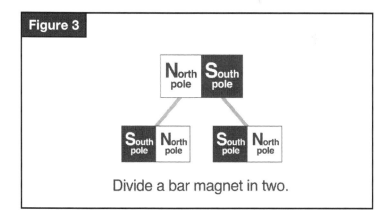

Divide a bar magnet in two.

5

Here's another example I often used in early seminars. It consists of a sheet of paper with the word *front* written on one side and *back* on the other. The moment we designate one side as the front, the back is born, and both sides exist in the same proportion.

It is the same for concepts such as strength and weakness. If we were to increase the strength, weakness would increase proportionally to the same extent, and if we were to reduce the weakness, the magnitude of the strength would diminish accordingly. We place value on increasing our strength, but strength and weakness are two sides of the same coin; the front and back form an inseparable pair. Perhaps this is something you understand from your own experience.

The bases of the double helix of DNA molecules are pairs. Additionally, it is my view that elementary particles (including particles and antiparticles, such as electrons and positrons) are pairs of polarities that spin in opposite directions. Even the smallest entities exist simultaneously as pairs. Energy is not born from just one single polarity. Matter is both created as a pair and annihilated as a pair.

Third-dimensional thought can only understand one side of these paired opposites. Since we have always seen everything as being divided, energy is dispersed. As a result, the true world has been obscured.

The two opposite polarities form a pair, just like the two sides of a coin, and exist simultaneously. To understand this, we need to observe from a specific position that enables us to overview everything from a high-dimensional domain.[2] Humans, who have lost sight of this point of view, stumble into a trap and become further ensnared as a result.

---

[2] For the purposes of this text, the word *overview* means to view from a high-dimensional domain.

Chapter 2

WHY THINGS ARE NOT THE WAY WE DESIRE

The World Is Reversed: The Trap of Reversal by Identification of Consciousness

Things don't go as you wish, and the more you chase after what you want, the further it moves away from you. This is because you have fallen into the trap of reversal of the third-dimensional world. Only when you escape this trap will you break the chain of repeating the same mistakes in life.

A radical turnaround awaits humanity. It begins when we understand our world's biggest deception: the trap of reversal. As you will see, everything before your eyes is reversed. Thus, you have never seen the truth at all. Once you accept this fact, you will understand why things haven't gone the way you wish, and inevitably, your life will change as a result.

We humans face all sorts of problems in our daily lives. Consider how much time and energy you spend resolving problems related to family, work, relationships, money, and health. Things may seem to improve a bit and go smoother for a while. But sooner or later, you realize that the same problems have simply changed form, only to reemerge and trouble you again and again. Try as you might, you never seem to reach a point where you feel satisfied. Why? Because, as stated previously, we humans live in a system where we cannot be 100 percent satisfied.

We cannot expect to simply find definitive solutions within the mechanisms of the third-dimensional world, which prevents us from seeing our problems for what they really are.

Let me discuss one example of these problems by introducing the system of reversal that has actually prevented your life from being fulfilling. The moment you identify one side as male, in this example, the other side becomes identified as female. The space generated between these two opposite polarities is what creates the trap of reversal. I also view that within the space between A and B—which were originally one but have been divided in two—there exists a rotary motion of energy suggested by a Möbius strip (see figure 4).

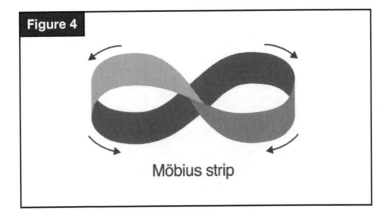

Figure 4

Möbius strip

As you may know, a Möbius strip is created by taking a length of material, giving it a half-twist, and joining the ends to form a loop. If you run your finger all the way along the outside surface of the strip, you end up on the inside of the strip—that is, the opposite side from where you began. If you continue along the strip, you return to the starting point. The front has become the back, and vice versa, as you move along the surface. The phenomenon symbolized in the Möbius strip happens inside our bodies as well as in our social environment.

My interpretation is that even inside the nucleus of an atom—the smallest core of your body—protons and neutrons are rotating rapidly in a Möbius-like motion. According to the yin-yang principle, when yin moves to its extreme polarity, it bounces back to yang, and vice versa. The relationship between you and the other person, or between you and any other phenomenon, is like the two sides of the same coin with a Möbius-like twist.

In other words, the world before your eyes is completely reversed. This is the truth of our world—and this is why even if you think you're moving forward, you are actually going back to the start. This may shock you and make you question what your life has been about until now—the life that you have tried so hard to live to the best of your abilities.

"It is not the universe but the earth that is rotating!" our ancestors discovered with great astonishment. The paradigm shift that I am describing, which is yet to come, is even more astounding, because it has elements that are closely linked to people's daily lives.

So how does this world create the phenomenon of reversal? As shown in figure 5, your own interior, like all phenomena, is divided in two. These two elements below your consciousness (A' and B') are in constant conflict. The letter A represents the directionality of the consciousness that is born from this conflict. This is called *identification*.

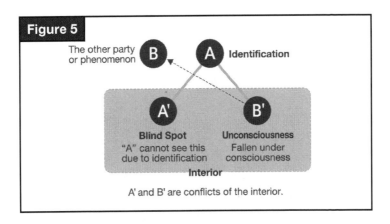

Figure 5

The other party or phenomenon **B** **A** Identification

A'
Blind Spot
"A" cannot see this due to identification

B'
Unconsciousness
Fallen under consciousness

Interior

A' and B' are conflicts of the interior.

When we shift our consciousness to one side of the divide, the unconsciousness in our interior is reversed outward. In the figure, this is represented by the letter B. In other words, what you cannot see in your interior is reflected in the person or phenomenon before you, as if you were viewing it projected on a movie screen. What is it, then, that we have actually been seeing this whole time?

Suppose you are trying very hard to have your efforts acknowledged by your company or spouse, to no effect. Even worse, you constantly experience unexpected failures and incidents that negate acknowledgment. You are simply doing what you think is right, even making extra efforts. However, there is a certain matter of which you are not aware: why must you try so hard to do what you have done?

Let us see what is happening in your interior. Inside you, there exist elements of two opposite polarities, such as feelings of inferiority and, on the other hand, confidence. Within this inner conflict, if confidence wins out over inferiority, you appear confident on the outside, and your sense of inferiority sinks below your consciousness. It is put into a state of unconsciousness.

Although you may act confident and try hard to appear so to your external environment, you are unaware that your sense of inferiority has not disappeared. Rather, you're benumbed by it. You have put a lid on the part of yourself that you do not want to see. But in truth, it is reversed outward, appearing as a person or phenomenon in your external environment. It is not your spouse or your company that does not acknowledge you—it is actually you who are not confident and always denying yourself.

If, on the other hand, your sense of inferiority wins out over your sense of confidence, someone capable or confident will manifest before your eyes. This may spur your feelings of inferiority, but there is no need to worry. You only see the reflection of what's inside you. You simply have to accept yourself as you are. If you can completely accept yourself as you are by looking at the other party, that capacity can be yours.

In other words, it does not matter whether you have feelings of inferiority or confidence, because what you see in the other person or phenomenon is just the superficial result of the conflict you have created in your interior. In our society, positive thinking is considered to be good, and so we tend to suppress negative thinking, always trying to shift toward the positive. However, the more we shift toward the positive, the more the suppressed negative emerges as a reversed phenomenon. This is the main reason things do not go well in life.

Since everything exists divided in two, the negative will not go away even if you are a positive thinker. Rather, when you strengthen the positive, the negative will grow in proportion.

You may argue that there are people who have become successful with a positive and forward-looking attitude. I will refer to this in detail later; for now, let me just say that they have become successful not because of their positive thinking, but because they know that *everything has already been accomplished.*

With third-dimensional thought, which shifts toward one side of two opposites, you will inevitably cause a phenomenon of reversal. This is why people who have gained status, reputation, and wealth by using their sense of inferiority or lack as the driving force often suddenly meet their downfall through some accidental problem. Though they may not show it on the surface, successful people know very well that they may endlessly face all sorts of problems such as betrayal or loss.

We always choose what we think is good and thus continue to strengthen those thoughts. At the same time, however, while seeking the realization of dreams, desires, and peace of mind, we unconsciously create a shift to their opposites in our interior, which we cannot ourselves see, including such negative elements as worry, fear, guilt, and doubt. Though many people perceive issues related to relationships, love, money, health, and so forth as problems, they are merely superficial phenomena.

The real problem is your unconsciousness and the fact that you have never realized that you are in it. The dreadful thing is that this unconsciousness engenders such phenomena with almighty power. Nothing can prevail against it in the third-dimensional world.

You may have noticed things that do not seem quite right, but you have never doubted whether the world you live in is functioning or not. But in truth, this world has been reversed fundamentally. The more you desire happiness, the unhappier you become. What you want is reversed and unattainable, and what you don't want to happen becomes reality. The more you become attached to something, the further it moves from you. Such is this system; it is a matter of course that things will not go well or will be painful.

There is no way for people or society to escape from self-contradictions, since we engage in love relationships, go about our work, and even conduct political and economic activities in the world of reversal.

What if we look at things in terms of a man or woman? Taking a basic example, a male identifies with the body of a man, and similarly, a female identifies with the body of a woman. However, as you see in figure 6, the interior of man and woman each contains maleness (father) and femaleness (mother), inherited from their parents.

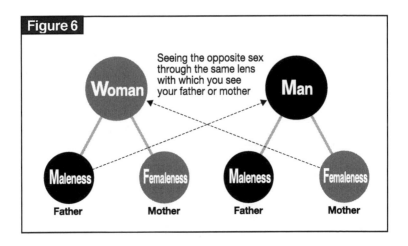

Figure 6

When you see a person of the opposite sex, you are seeing the reflection of the opposite sex in your interior being reversed onto the person. In short, you see the opposite sex through the same lens with which you see your father or mother.

What is being reflected in your husband? It is the same quality that you see in your father: perhaps a person who is stubborn, indecisive, and does not listen to his children, along with good traits, such as being kind and dependable. This occurs even if your father died when you were a child and you feel you never knew him; if lonely feelings result, what is reflected onto your husband is a person who makes you lonely.

If a husband did not like his mother and chose a woman with qualities he believed to be the complete opposite of hers, sooner or later, he would find that his wife had become just like his mother. Even if he divorced her and remarried a totally different type of woman, eventually he will end up in the same marriage pattern. Haven't you already experienced something like this? When identification occurs and a man identifies with the body of a man, or a woman with the body of a woman, the opposite sex within his or her interior is reversed and appears in his or her exterior. This is why you end up following the same path as your parents and become entangled in the same chain of events, no matter how much you dislike it.

Let's take, for example, a wife who strongly hopes for her husband's success. Like many women who seek kindness and dependability in their men, she married this man out of attraction to his dependability as well as his future potential. At first, everything seemed headed in the right direction. However—perhaps when the husband received an unfavorable evaluation from his employer—his attitude started to change. He began to appear less motivated and instead looked enviously at other people's promotions.

She tried to encourage him, but the situation did not change, and her irritation grew. She then remembered that her father was weak-willed and her mother was constantly complaining. She had grown to hate the kind of relationship her parents had and thus had chosen a person she thought was reliable.

But the problem was not with her husband. It was the maleness in her. Because she had an unreliable maleness in her interior, she was always criticizing him, saying, "That's what's no good about you" or "You won't succeed that way." As a result, she depleted the vitality out of him. Her husband, who had been her ideal at the beginning, was reversed to become an unreliable person, in accordance with the system.

This example is not the exception. In the world of reversal, you step on the accelerator of "want to be" while simultaneously pushing on the brake of "cannot be"—and end up creating a situation in which things cannot go forward.

Human beings have repeatedly made efforts to end battles and become unified as one. But if we try to be unified in our external environment, our efforts will go unrewarded as long as we have conflicts in our interior. It is therefore impossible to become unified as one in a true sense in the world of division, where we fall into the trap of reversal. If it were possible, the world would have changed a long time ago.

Reversal of consciousness and Reversal by Identification with the body are the true causes of things not going as we wish. You may already be familiar with the term *reversal* or a similar concept in Eastern teachings; this term suggests that your inner aspects are reflected as outer phenomena, or similarly, that the inside of the earth is reversed as the outside. Unless we understand the concept of reversal at the level of everyday life and know how to deal with it, it ends up being mere information. As a result, we are compelled to remain as we are.

Since the reality of reversal has now become clear, however, there is no longer any need for us to remain as we are. I will now describe, in a concrete manner, how to escape from the world of reversal.

Chapter 3

ESCAPE FROM THE WORLD OF REVERSAL

Shifting Gears to Dimensional Displacement through Dual-Structured Coexistence

Once you understand the Miross system, your situation will change instantaneously. Even problems so difficult that you have given up on them will disappear. By gaining a high-dimensional viewpoint, you will be able to escape from the third-dimensional world, which is bound by limitations.

Having lost sight of the position that allows us to overview everything, we humans have fallen into a trap. This means we will be able to escape the trap if we can attain this overview position.

The diagram in figure 7, which I always use when I talk about Miross, shows the high-dimensional symmetrical system. This diagram is very simple; yet it contains perfection, harmony, and all the systems of human beings.

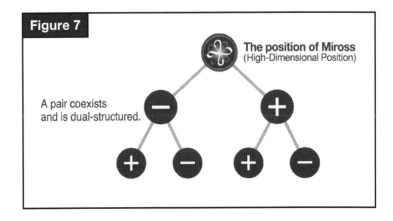

The position from which you overview is a dimensionally displaced position—a high-dimensional position that transcends the third dimension—and it shows that a pair, when overviewed from the high-dimensional domain, both coexists and is dual-structured. I call this *Dual-Structured Coexistence*. Both the subject and the object are the same. Opposite polarities—such as micro and macro, past and future, space and matter, and inside and outside—are all the same.

Having forgotten this high-dimensional position, we humans have stumbled blindly and unwittingly into the world of reversal. With my insight, I was able to elucidate the human structure using the system of Dual-Structured Coexistence. I am convinced that it is now possible for all people to demystify and initialize their lives on their own.

At the same time, this discovery indicates the directionality of evolution, which goes far beyond the framework of the conventional human system. Human beings have engaged in repeated disputes between different ethnic groups for thousands of years and have never managed to end this cycle. We get caught in a loop of happiness and unhappiness and never feel fulfilled in our lives.

We cannot find solutions to the root problems of social ills while we continue down this spiraling path of aggravation. It can be firmly said that the world we hope for can never exist as an extension of our current path. We need to transcend the conventional human system with courage and determination. This is what it means to shift gears to dimensionally displaced thought, which affords us the overview of Dual-Structured Coexistence.

Society has progressed rapidly by replacing the human brain with the computer. This was possible through the availability of this revolutionary invention to virtually anyone. How, then, can we make methods of human evolution available to anyone? Together with my wife, I have developed practical methods to do exactly this by demystifying the human structure using the model of the ultimate paired opposites: man and woman.

These methods, being the essence of a high-dimensional system, are normally difficult to grasp. We have therefore made it possible for everyone to experience them in daily life by using a familiar concept that anyone can relate to: the physical entities of man and woman. If, in fact, human beings exist as a perfect system of Dual-Structured Coexistence, we can escape from our current situations by making use of this system.

When you understand the Miross system, you will attain a position from which you can overview whatever kind of life you have led and any events that have occurred. From this position, when you apply the system to any phenomenon or emotion you experience, you will begin to see your thought patterns and become able to remove yourself from the present state to which you are tethered by your emotions. Once your understanding reaches a level where you accept your long-term worries and sufferings with an *aha*-like moment—when you recognize, "Oh, *that's* how it was!"—phenomena will start changing as if chemical reactions had occurred.

Divided in two (as we are), we humans have so far lived as only one side of the two in a world that we have created based on our assumptions. As I said previously, all we see is the reflection of our interior reversed out to the external environment. Therefore, our assumptions are extremely rigid, as if locked inside. As long as you have assumptions like "this person is such-and-such a way" or "this is absolutely impossible," you will be unable to see real life.

Moreover, whenever you think about yourself, especially when you are alone, you don't tend to dwell on your charms or positive aspects. Most of your thoughts, such as worries and fear, are negative. Those elements that you unconsciously repeat are reversed and eventually become actualized.

This is why you need to carefully observe your thought patterns and the words you habitually repeat. If you can observe these patterns objectively, you will begin to notice how easily your thoughts become entrapped by them and end up running in circles. If you clearly recognize and erase your assumptions, as well as the phenomena seen through the patterns of your thoughts, the landscape around you will change completely.

What is so remarkable about this system is that once you understand it, phenomena change in a flash. It is a system, and thus, like a computer, it does not take time to work.

Your mother-in-law who has long treated you badly or your supervisor who has been excessively harsh will suddenly start speaking to you with care and appreciation the moment you understand them through the system. A tyrannical husband will change completely, becoming kind as never before. Financial problems that seemed deadlocked will be resolved simply and impossibly. You'll read some detailed examples in the case studies described in chapter 9 and discover how you can experience phenomena like these—almost laughingly, in the blink of an eye.

Even with a rudimentary understanding of the system, you can be released from the stalemate in your external environment. With a deeper understanding of the system, however, and by applying the methods consistently, you will unfailingly actualize an initialization and complete regeneration of life.

This high-dimensional symmetrical system represents the super-balanced state of "all is one." But once an energy force, such as emotion or thought, is input, the switch turns on, and the system is activated. This is the mechanism through which, as soon as identification takes place, reversal occurs.

The way to escape from the trap of reversal is to reverse the vector (that is, the directional energy) that you initially directed toward the other party and return it to your interior. This is the application of the Miross system.

The world we live in is already reversed. To reverse what has already been reversed is to return it to its true origin. As a result, new space emerges, which is high-dimensional space. I therefore call this *High-Dimensional Space by Reversal with Anti-vector.*

The illusory world that your reversed consciousness has created starts to transform into a real world. Many people who have experienced this transformation recount that their problems have simply vanished. This readily demonstrates that the problems themselves were merely illusions created by their own misconceptions or assumptions.

Throughout your life, your thoughts have always been directed toward others—your counterparts or other parties. You've been saying, "I can't forgive this facet of my husband" or "I don't like that aspect of my supervisor," and so on. This vector of consciousness that you feel toward the other party should be redirected to you as an anti-vector. In short, the reversed phenomenon that you see is yours, so you simply bring it back to its place of origin. This is the crux of the Miross system. But why, you may wonder, do your problems vanish as a result? I will explain this in figure 8.

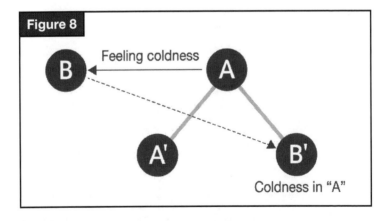

Let us assume that you are person A and that you feel distressed when you detect coldness in person B. In this case, the coldness in the interior of A (B) is reversed outward and reflected in B.

Now if you, A, bring the coldness back to yourself, (A' and B') will be "pair-annihilated," and A (which is you, or more precisely, your manifested ego) will also be annihilated. As the person who is looking (that is, A) disappears, A is energetically annihilated and vanishes. The person who is looked at (that is, B) simultaneously vanishes energetically as well, along with the coldness that was manifested previously. This is the mechanism.

Thus our egos, engendered as a result of living on only one side of the two opposite polarities, are annihilated. Since it is not simply hidden or masked but truly annihilated, once that which has been reversed outward is returned inward, it will never again be reversed outward.

The nonreversible world is sure and sustainable. Here, we need never fear failure or intimidation from outside ourselves, because we no longer need to try to change anyone or fight with others. Furthermore, we will encounter something that humans have never experienced until now.

What is that coldness, mentioned earlier, that is in your interior? It is a sensation of coldness you have toward your external environment, meaning toward another person. In returning everything to yourself, you need to realize that the coldness you feel toward someone else is in fact something inside of you. It is not the coldness of the other person; rather, you are the one who has been cold to yourself. This is a new viewpoint from which you see yourself witnessing the coldness and understanding what it really is. This is the true picture of the coldness in your interior, which could not have been seen without attaining the Miross position.

From this position, for the first time ever, you can overview and get a sense of your relationship with yourself. The conventional concept of relationship emerges only through the existence of other people or beings separate and different from you. Therefore, all of your consciousness has been directed toward others. You judge everything based on others or how you are seen and perceived by them. This is how life has been, and everything originates from here. Your emotions, mind, things you thought were yours were all a virtual you—that is, your ego—created by others.

Now the "you" whom you have seen through the eyes of others can reclaim its own viewpoint. For the first time, you can direct your eyes toward yourself. This means that for the very first time, you have proof of your own existence.

How has such a thing become possible? It is through the discovery of the position from which everything can be overviewed. The position of Miross awakens human beings who have thus far identified themselves with their physical bodies. It has opened the door for them to escape the world of optical illusions. Dual-Structured Coexistence is, in fact, a dissection map of human relationships. Let us demystify our thought process (see figure 9).

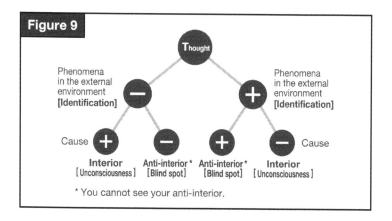

As I mentioned previously, we humans have a belief in and directionality toward positive thinking. What kind of world is this? If you exude the positive in your external environment, the other polarity naturally becomes negative. Whether our interiors seem positive or negative in our minds, our interiors are made up of both these polarities, which are essentially the same as each other. Interestingly, positive thinking hides the negative under the unconsciousness; similarly, negative thinking hides the positive.

Just as when, while carrying a heavy bag in one hand, we unconsciously shift our weight to the other side, humans naturally create balance. Negative thinkers actually have the positive—a sense of security—deep in their interior, and this is why they can remain in a state of negative thinking. Being in the negative, they can avoid a variety of unwanted incidents. Who would have imagined that this happens thanks to the unconsciously hidden positive? Because humans cannot see the whole picture, we jump to the shortsighted conclusion that positive is good and negative is bad. This prevents us from finding our way out of the maze.

From the position of Miross, our distorted eyes, which have seen the external environment as a world divided in two, will be replaced with new eyes capable of overviewing the entire picture. This will change everything you see. From here on, I would like to discuss some concrete examples that show how you can apply this system to your daily life.

Chapter 4

ATTAINING A POSITION TO OVERVIEW YOUR LIFE

Everything Is Based on the Relationship to the Self

All problems are created by you in the mechanism of the relationship system. The moment you understand this, the cause of your problems will disappear, and your situation will change dramatically. You will never again be fooled by the trap of the third-dimensional world.

The world we see is quite obscure. You may think, *This is how I am* or *This is how you are,* but your perception of yourself often changes depending on someone else's identity or position—that is, based on your relationship with the other person. Where, then, is the real you?

Take another look at figure 7.

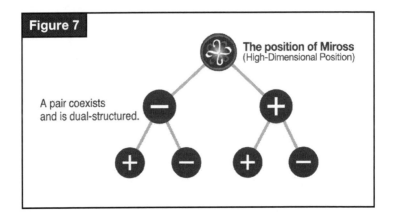

As you apply the system shown in the figure to various cases, you will begin to see every relationship multidimensionally and understand that the system indeed operates accurately.

Let's examine this mechanism in a more concrete fashion. Everyone knows that man and woman are a pair. But think how much more interesting this idea would be if I told you that anything you cannot see in yourself is hidden in your partner, and unlimited energy can be switched on between the pair of you just as electricity lights up when you put plus and minus together.

As you can see in figure 7, when you place yourself as one of the pair (in the diagram, the large plus or minus), two polarities (the small plus and minus) appear in you, and another two appear in the other party—all of which are in fact you, though totally unknown to you. It is your partner, one half of the pair, who can reveal these hidden polarities—that is, your interior—more clearly than anyone else by projecting your reversed interior onto herself or himself.

Let's imagine an ordinary couple. The wife thought that everything was going well, but suddenly she finds out that her husband is having an affair. She believes that she truly loves her husband and has dedicated herself to him, but now she feels lost, as if plunged into darkness. She suffers great pain, as she feels betrayed and unloved. What, then, is being reversed outward and reflected in her external environment? The unconsciousness inside of her shows that it is she who does not love herself; it is she who is betraying herself by not loving herself. But because her senses are numb to this fact, it is impossible for her to realize that she doesn't love her own self. That is why she tried to maintain a balance by loving and dedicating herself to her husband. This unseen part of herself, in turn, was exposed like a bolt from the blue through her husband's affair.

How does it look from the husband's perspective? He does not think there is any love at all inside of him. That is why he seeks love in his external environment, constantly striving to confirm its existence. But because he doesn't truly understand love and is thus only capable of selfish love, he begins to have feelings toward other women who can make him feel loved instead of his dedicated wife.

What happens to the wife when she realizes on the deepest level that the problem was not her husband after all, but her own inability to love herself? As we will discuss in more detail later in the text, the world surrounding you is your own individual universe. Once she understands clearly that an incident in which she felt unloved actually occurred because she does not love herself, the incident itself will be reset, and she will begin to see a new universe. The husband, being one of the pair, sees that the femaleness within himself is revived. He can feel the love that has always been inside of him and begins to be able to love himself. As a result, he returns to his wife, who exudes fresh attractiveness because she has started loving herself.

As shown in this example, once the understanding of the relationship system between the pair deepens, their "why" questions will be easily demystified and answered. *Why do your children have problems? Why do you have conflicts with your parents-in-law? Why do you keep having problems with money? Why doesn't your work go as you wish?*

Impossible as it may seem, married couples who have become nearly strangers to each other—even those who have been through terrible experiences such as domestic violence—can return to being the couples they once were, destined to meet and be happy, once they see through the illusions they have created due to the trap of reversal. It is as if withered plants and trees, seemingly perishing, are revived.

As mentioned previously, if a pair coexists and is dual-structured, it means the subject and object are the same. By applying what I call "the system," you can begin to dissect the situations and emotions that arise from any relationship between subject and object, such as marriage partners or lovers, parents and children, and supervisor and employee, as well as your relationship with money, health, and other factors.

We humans always try to justify our behavior and speech; this is why we fight with others. But when you understand your behavior based on the system, you will discover that the reasons for such behavior actually arose from somewhere completely unexpected.

While it is rather easy to imagine the relationship system with other people, it may be more difficult to understand it with material items such as money. Money is a material item, but the worry and pain generated by money are emotions, which are subject to the same mechanism that occurs between two people.

Here is an example. You work hard to earn money, but your circumstances do not improve, or they start to go well but then worsen again. You cannot get out of a financial situation in which you feel you never have enough money. You think if only you had enough money, you could achieve your dream—but your dream seems to move further and further away.

What is hidden in the unconsciousness of someone like this? You have suppressed the negative thoughts and hateful feelings about money that originated in your childhood when you saw your parents suffering from financial problems. Within you, there is a sense of not having enough or not deserving to have money. And precisely because of these feelings, you have a strong attachment to money and make extra effort to obtain more. These feelings are reversed and reflected in money, and as a result, money continues to move away from you.

Sentiments toward money are as strong and deep as those toward love. You may not be aware of this, but they control your daily life by way of powerful restrictions. If you can more clearly understand your relationship with money, financial matters that have been stagnant will begin to flow, whether that means you receive a job offer, get a raise, or experience increased sales. As you witness these changes related to money, you will realize that you have been the one standing in the way.

Dealing with Social Problems

Once you know the system, you can free yourself from any social problems—such as domestic violence, depression, bullying, and divorce—without depending on anyone else. Here are a few examples.

Bullying

In the example of bullying, the subject is the one who inflicts the bullying, and the object is the one being bullied. In truth, though, both have elements of bullying and being bullied in their interiors.

The offender bullies because he sees himself in the victim, and he cannot stand seeing this abominable part of himself, which he has suppressed. However, due to the phenomenon of identification, whereby he identifies with the offender, there is no way for him to know that he has the victim in his interior. The perpetrator does not know why he bullies, nor does he know that the victim is himself. The more he bullies, the more he hurts himself.

What about the victim? Like the wife discussed previously, he is the one inflicting pain upon himself. He dislikes himself, and this unconscious thought that he is worthless and should never have been born is reversed outward. Thus, he ends up being bullied. Like the bully, he cannot imagine the reason he is bullied, nor can he see that he is actually an offender, hurting himself.

What the other party does to you is actually what you are doing to yourself; likewise, what you do to the other person is what you do to yourself. In effect, both parties are bullying.

It may seem merciless, even daring, to say that the offender and victim are the same, especially when we consider the feelings of parents whose children have committed suicide after going through vast emotional pain and suffering. However, this is all the more reason that we cannot afford to turn our eyes away from the true picture of the situation. I am not suggesting that the offender bears no responsibility. But this is not the point.

If we understand the mechanism of bullying, we can prevent it, and those who are victimized can escape their situations. I sincerely hope we can put an end to such tragedies. In fact, there are cases of children who, having been bullied to the point where they refused to go to school, came to understand the system on their own and overcame the bullying. As a result, they not only were able to return to school, but also in some cases became tremendously popular among their peers. It is the same with bullying among adults, though children who have yet to be fully immersed in the rules of the third-dimensional world are quicker to understand the system and change, compared with adults who have long been bound by such rules.

Depression

It is said that an increasing number of people suffer from depression, the causes and symptoms of which vary. If we take the example of social withdrawal, we can examine it in the following way.

Among those who, for whatever reasons, have become socially withdrawn, there are many cases where people have become so sensitive toward others and the circumstances surrounding them that they cannot even step out of their houses. They suffer because they cannot help but hide in their shells. They do not realize, though, that there is an innate advantage for them in shutting themselves up in their own world. Perhaps they do not want to do the work they despise. If they stay in their own world, avoiding contact with others, they are comfortable and can depend upon their parents and family members. But these reasons to remain in their current state must contend with their desire to come out of it.

The fact that they confine themselves in their own world does not mean they do not have any relationship with the outside world whatsoever. In fact, resisting the outside world means that such a relationship already exists. Even people who do not work, have no contact with family members, and connect with no one suffer from mental agony because of their relationship with the external environment. Thoughts such as *No one accepts me as I am* or *There is no place for me* are generated from the relationship with one's own self.

If they can see what other people are to them and exactly what the phenomena that fall upon them are, they will realize how comical it is to have fought with the illusion—that is, the external environment—that they created by confining themselves in their rooms. Once they can see all this, the door of the room will open automatically, and they will be able to exit it.

Domestic Violence

Domestic violence is another serious social problem. People often think that there is nothing for a victim to do other than somehow escape from the perpetrator or resort to legal action. Yet we have encountered cases such as the following.

A woman who could no longer put up with her husband's violence ran away from him, taking her children with her. She moved from place to place, hiding from him, and finally came to us, desperately seeking help from the Miross system. The abuse perpetrated by her husband was in fact not her first experience of this kind of violence. She had also been a victim of abuse by her father as well as her schoolteacher. But only when she found herself raising her own hand to her children did she, who had suffered from abuse for so many years, come to the point of mental breakdown.

Her understanding of the Miross system grew in proportion to her desire to be saved, and as she applied the system, she went through drastic changes. She saw in her partner a deep, pressing, almost violent sense of lack that desperately cried out for acceptance. She saw with clarity a suffering for never having been loved. She then came to understand that because she too possessed this sense of lack and suffering, she had attracted a partner with the same qualities. Simply by becoming aware of this, she no longer put herself in a position to bring abuse upon herself. There was, therefore, no longer any reason for her to be abused. With the relief that came from dissolving the strain of so many years, her life underwent a great change.

The change did not stop with her. Her husband, who also practiced Miross, experienced great change as well, and they were able to restore their marital relationship. As unimaginable as it may seem, the couple's bond is now even deeper than when they were first married, and they are enjoying a regenerated life with their children. Similarly, their children, who grew up seeing violence between their parents and have experienced bullying in their own lives, have seen their situation change.

As you come to understand the system, you will realize that the phenomena that happen to you simply originate from you. As a result, you will no longer be swayed by anything external. You could say, in other words, that you can no longer blame anyone or anything as you did before.

In truth, this can be agonizing for those who are very much used to the conventional human program. It is much easier to blame someone else. But which would you choose: a life in which problems follow you to the end, or a life you can live as you wish? If you truly understand that you can make anything happen as you wish, you will be liberated from the human program and have freedom in hand.

There is one thing here you should pay particular attention to: when you understand that phenomena originate from you, you may tend to blame yourself. You may feel distressed or guilty, wonder what is wrong with you, or feel hatred toward your parents for making you the way you are. The truth is that your parents and their parents had to live this way because they, like you, were caught in the world of the uncontrollable trap called division and reversal. Nothing was wrong with you or them. We have simply been trifled with by the trap of the human program. What appears before your eyes is nothing more than your interior and the system.

I hope that you will be able to overview your life and start afresh by using this new human software. I feel deeply moved whenever I encounter people who have been liberated from harsh lives and painful experiences. They can even laugh at the past, saying, "Oh, that's just how it was." They realize that their lives were the way they were programmed to be—that they were simply acting as themselves in a drama they had written. Intelligence with which you are able to observe your life in totality from an objective point of view is proof of human evolution.

Chapter 5

LIBERATING THE HIDDEN, UNEXPERIENCED ZONE BETWEEN MAN AND WOMAN

Partnerunity: The Truth of Man and Woman

In the third-dimensional world, the truth between man and woman has always been concealed. But when you apply this system with your partner, your very existence, which has been hidden, will become clear. As two opposite polarities, a man and woman become a perfect core after fusion—and a new time and space, never before experienced, is born.

What is self? In the third-dimensional world, where everything is divided in two, even the self is divided in two. In fact, the Japanese characters for *self*—自分 *(jibun)*—literally mean "dividing a self."

Another word for *self* consists of four Japanese characters: 自分自身 *(jibun-jishin)*. When these characters are interpreted literally, they mean "your own body that you yourself have divided." A self therefore refers to you, comprising yourself plus your other self. This indicates that there exists the opposite polarity of you: your partner.

Man and woman as a pair are one. This is the most basic principle for humans. It may, however, also be the most difficult to understand. This is because the existence of the two opposite polarities that form a pair has been hidden, as discussed previously in this text.

To reiterate, if we wish to continue to live within the conventional human program, there is no need for us to understand the fact that we are actually divided in two—that the other half of a person's pair, with whom he or she was originally one, exists. We could just set that idea aside, viewing it as nothing more than a romantic illusion of youth, destined to vanish in despair.

But this time, it's different. In fact, in terms of human evolution and existence, this is the most critical matter there is. We cannot afford to ignore it any longer.

In order to replace human daily life with the high-dimensional symmetrical system, my partner and I have systematized the real-life experiences that unfold between man and woman as two opposite polarities. We have constructed a system in such a way that anyone, under any circumstances, can apply it to his or her own life.

At the time of the system's completion, we felt that by using it, humans would be liberated from all suffering and people would come to understand that further human evolution was indeed possible. And so, with great enthusiasm, we began our crusade.

However, in Japan, this notion of man and woman was at first the very factor that stood in our way of promoting Miross. In particular, people who were focused on seeking success did not understand or find meaning in the concept of partnership, and we came up against numerous walls of resistance. Today this idea is more accepted, and there seems to be less resistance to it.

Even when people vaguely accepted the notion of man and woman as a pair, doubts seemed to arise as soon as they were told that man and woman are a pair of the same nature. Worse, no one was willing to even lend an ear to the idea of being one with her or his spouse.

Problems stemming from the relationship between men and women are a fact of everyday life. When it comes to marital relationships, the initial passion of love fades over time. Who, then, could ever imagine that the key to the evolution of humankind could be found there? Young people, who yearn for love and romance, see hope and dreams in marriage, but they do not understand the true state or meaning of man and woman. When they look at the adults around them, they cannot see the reality or potential of love.

However, some people truly want to change and experience the world they have envisioned during their lifetimes. They have tried the system and proven beautifully that when they applied it, the problems surrounding them vanished with certainty. They were able to have new experiences they had never anticipated. What is the truth, then, hidden between man and woman?

I sometimes explain the world of paired opposites using the analogy of a mirror. We need other people as mirrors in order to see ourselves. However, the common notion that the person you see before you is also a mirror of yourself is often mistakenly interpreted to mean that the negative part of you is being reflected, and that self-reflection is needed. Unless you clearly understand that the subject and object are two mirrors held against each other, you will not truly understand. Self-awareness and self-reflection alone do not lead to solving problems at their root.

Take another look at figure 9.

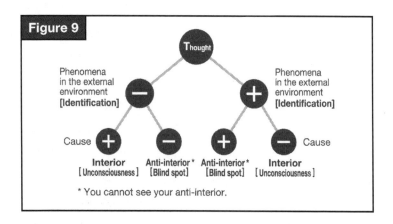

You can see that your interior contains both unconsciousness and a blind spot. When two mirrors are held facing each other, you begin to see four unseen parts of the world: your front and back, and those of your partner. Only when you are able to see all of these will you know your true self, which you were unable to discover no matter how much you tried. It is the true meaning of who you are. With two mirrors facing each other, you see your front and back; when you do so, the world as you have perceived and understood it will crumble, and an entirely new world will unfold before your eyes. Through the fusion of the two opposite polarities within you—namely, maleness and femaleness—balance is achieved. I call this marriage balance. And marriage balance means being *arugamama* (あるがまま), or "you being as you are."

Typically, people say "you being as you are" as a simple affirmation, meaning that something may be lacking, missing, or even wrong with you but it is still okay to be you, just the way you are. However, this is not what I mean by *arugamama* here. Rather, you exist as you are by overviewing yourself from a high-dimensional domain. Without understanding the system, even when you affirm the present self as you are, you do so in a way that affirms what is lacking as well. As a result, sooner or later, these negatives will emerge on the surface. *Arugamama* neither affirms nor negates. It is simply you being in harmony, borne out of the understanding that you already are in perfect harmony, as overviewed from a high-dimensional position.

If, as a husband or wife, you complete a marriage balance, thereby becoming as you are, you can transform your spouse into an ideal partner. Likewise, if you are single, you can attract an ideal partner. We will explore this idea in greater detail elsewhere.

From here, we enter an amazing world of two mirrors facing each other. To be able to see all of yourself is to eliminate the world of illusion that you created based on your assumptions and instead establish the reality of your existence as a true self.

Some people fear the idea of knowing themselves. They may not want to see their unfathomable darkness, or they fear what may come out of it. But this is only because they are deceived by the illusion that has unfolded in the world of reversal, which they have created. The only thing you will find by totally eliminating your inner conflicts is the world of absolute peace. This is the domain reached by transcending the third-dimensional world of division.

Up to this point, we have been unable to live as our true selves, because consciousness has not yet been formed in the third-dimensional world. It has remained reversed, drifting about without converging. In order to live as you wish, you must create true consciousness that will never be reversed.

How then can we produce true consciousness in a world divided in two? In the first place, because consciousness is confined within the human body, it is impossible for humans to observe themselves objectively. It may seem as though we are doing so, but actually, we observe ourselves from just one side.

Directing consciousness toward an object is a state in which the vector is directed toward the other party. This means division; it is the third-dimensional world of "you and I are different." When you bring the vector back toward yourself, this is the beginning of fusion: "You and I are the same." This is the essence of the application of Miross. You may be bewildered at first as you try to grasp a concept that is totally foreign to you. But the fact that you are divided in two means that your consciousness is also divided into two. As shown in figure 10, your consciousness also exists in the other party. This is why your attitude and feelings change depending on the person with whom you are relating. Essentially, there is no true existence of yourself in relationships.

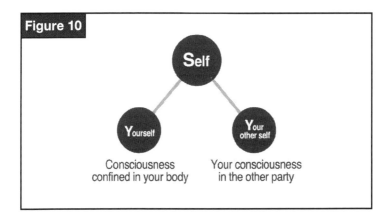

You can become aware of your own unconsciousness if you apply the system of Reversal by Identification. But if in fact you (the subject) exist in the other party (the object), the existence of a partner is essential for you to complete yourself (*jibun-jishin* 自分自身). The front side of you can only be seen by the other party. In short, a human can only understand herself or himself as manifested on the surface through the eyes of the other party. Your partner is the one who can show the unseen part of you clearer than anyone else, just as you can do for your partner.

The things you have fought against, thinking they were caused by the other party, will subside only when you come to understand that your own interior is actually the cause. That which you despised or suppressed is, in fact, the energy source that drove you to action. It was an act performed by you and your other self—that is, an act entirely of your own creation.

Through the other party, you can fulfill what has been lacking and erase unnecessary illusions. When one-directional consciousness becomes two-directional, balance is achieved, and everything falls into place in a state of super-balance. The two will become whole when four kinds of recognition are unified into one through the system of Dual-Structured Coexistence. When this occurs, you can achieve true consciousness for the first time.

Unifying these four kinds of recognition signifies a grand *weltanschauung* (comprehensive worldview). The nucleobases of DNA (adenine, guanine, cytosine, thymine) as well as blood types (A, B, O, AB) are all composed of four types. The interaction of the natural world also comprises four forces: gravity, electromagnetic force, strong nuclear force, and weak nuclear force. This is no mere coincidence; rather, it is my belief that this symbolic number of energy elements controls all matter.

This concept of unifying yourself with your partner is what I call partnerunity. You can see your unconsciousness reflected in your partner. But how can you see your blind spot, which was created by identification? To do that, you will need your partner's assistance. As shown in figure 11, your blind spot will clearly surface by interchanging the you (the small plus sign below the large minus sign) seen by your partner (the you of the external environment, represented by the large minus sign) with the you (small minus sign below large plus sign) that exists in your partner as seen by you (large plus sign, as seen by the large minus sign).

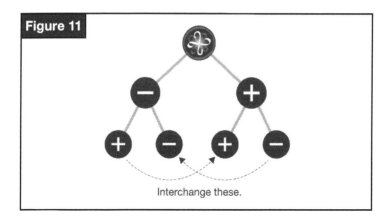

Figure 11

Interchange these.

By doing this, what you thought were aspects of your partner prove to be a part of your consciousness. What you thought was you proves to be part of your partner's consciousness. Thus, the concept of your own body that you yourself have divided becomes much more real. As inner conflicts begin to disappear, the boundary between you and your partner will also vanish, and true existence, unified as one, will surface.

What will be created by a man who has achieved a marriage balance and a woman who has done the same? The answer can be expressed through the following equation: (1) + (-1) = 0. In other words, one with plus energy added to the other with minus energy does not become one. Rather, it becomes zero, or space of infinite energy. As you may infer from the physiology of man and woman, maleness represents the energy of divergence, while femaleness represents the energy of convergence.

You may have seen the geometrical figure of a torus, which represents the energy flow of the universe. As shown in figure 12, energy diffuses outward, is reversed, and then converges inward.

If we interpret the concept further, a man is a living organism representing space, and a woman is that which represents time.

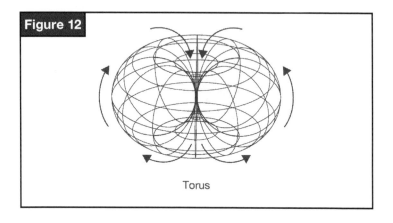

Figure 12

Torus

From the position of Miross, to draw forth your unconsciousness with eyes that view others means to create a new space that has been re-reversed from the world of reversal. Between a man and a woman who have achieved their partnerunity, new space and time, or High-Dimensional Space, is generated. In this space, it is possible for a man and woman who have become a perfect core of the smallest unit to create absolutely any world they wish through the fusion of opposite polarities, just as they can create new life. Thus far in our lives, we have been able to choose only from that which is already created. With partnerunity, we enter into an entirely new domain of creation.

While I cannot predict the probability of specific adult couples getting married, I am certain that when coupled individuals apply the system with their partners, they will discover the mechanism that attracted them to each other, and they will understand that their meeting was not an accident but rather meant to happen with the highest probability. This meeting is like an unexpected encounter with yourself, and I do not exaggerate when I say that it is like a thrilling treasure hunt.

The person you love, being the opposite polarity, is the one who will show you the parts of yourself that you despise the most. Through partnerunity, normal couples change the space between themselves in their daily life, creating a space of dynamic energy. It is like magic that turns poison into honey.

A world that far surpasses the life they have lived so far will start to unfold for any couple, just as it did for my partner and me. This is the *weltanschauung:* the truth of man and woman that is hidden in the third-dimensional world.

Figure 13 shows the origin of creation born out of maleness and femaleness. The system has nothing to do with any religion. However, to illustrate my point more clearly, let us imagine Adam as maleness and Eve as femaleness.

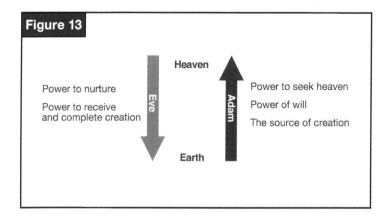

Figure 13

Heaven

Power to nurture

Power to receive
and complete creation

Eve

Adam

Power to seek heaven

Power of will

The source of creation

Earth

Adam is the origin of creation and represents the power to seek heaven, while Eve represents the power to nurture and complete creation. In other words, the origin of creation can be likened to a sperm that directs itself with great determination toward unlimited potential, reaching one ovum that receives and nurtures it. With these two powers, all matter in the third-dimensional world was created.

The source of human beings, which was born from man and woman, has long been neglected, and the memory of the high-dimensional domain has been lost. We humans are nevertheless born into the third-dimensional world through a man and a woman, and only through the partnerunity of the man and the woman will we evolve to a high-dimensional world. When the concept of man and woman takes root in our daily lives, it will be recognized as a unity that encompasses a cosmic view.

Chapter 6

LIVING DYNAMICALLY BY UNDERSTANDING THE TRUTH ABOUT PAST AND FUTURE

High-Dimensional Space by Reversal with
Anti-vector and the Trap of Time and Space

High-Dimensional Space by Reversal with Anti-vector—the true world that has transcended the domain of the third-dimensional world—is a magnificent field of creation beyond anything you have imagined. In this space, which comprises everything and includes at once the past and the future, you will be able to create your life dynamically.

A radical turnaround awaits people who have been able to escape from the world of reversal. We can transition smoothly through this turnaround while we are still alive. This is High-Dimensional Space by Reversal with Anti-vector: high-dimensional space created by bringing a vector back to yourself from the object. This space dispels conventional concepts of the third dimension—but it has, in fact, always been the true world.

I will discuss one more significant trap that humans have fallen into: the trap of time and space.

Up until the present day, common sense has dictated that a timeline goes to the future through the present, coming from the past. However, as you might have noticed in your reading thus far, in the reversed space with the returned vector, there exists time that flows from the future simultaneously.

In the third-dimensional world, where we have lived shifting toward one or the other side of two opposite polarities, the present is based on data from the past. Even if we project the future, it is simply a reprint of the past—in other words, looking at the past from the past. In fact, the future does not exist in the place where you perceive it to exist according to your present thoughts. One could say that in High-Dimensional Space by Reversal with Anti-vector, a new stage is being prepared for each and every being to restart his or her life.

As shown in figure 14, in the space formed by two vectors— one from the past to the future, and the other from the future to the past—a place called the "Now" is created. The Now is not a moment on a timeline that comes from the past and simply flows into the future; it is space that encompasses the past, the future, and all matter. This expanse of space is true time.

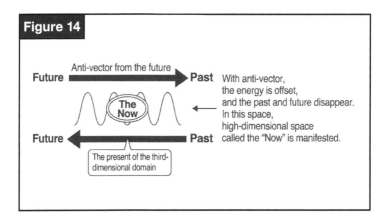

Figure 14

Anti-vector from the future

Future ➡ Past

The Now

Future ⬅ Past

The present of the third-dimensional domain

With anti-vector, the energy is offset, and the past and future disappear. In this space, high-dimensional space called the "Now" is manifested.

The past has not yet passed, and the future is not yet to come. All are already here.

Let's take a look at time and space composed of Dual-Structured Coexistence. As soon as you recall the past, it becomes the present for the you in the past and exists simultaneously with the present you—that is, the one who recalls the past. Furthermore, the present in which you imagine the future and the future you imagine are both the present for you and exist simultaneously. This means the you of the Now can speak to the you of the past and even receive an intuitive message as an inspiration from the accomplished you of the future.

In this space, wouldn't you then be able to freely control regrets from the past, memories that continue to make you suffer, or dreams and thoughts of how you want to be in the future? Through the application of Miross, you can even modify the deeply ingrained assumptions you have had in the past and thus repaint the past, transcending time and space. Here is an example.

A woman had been hurt by her parents' divorce when she was young. Because her father had abandoned her by leaving the family, she felt hatred toward him that she could not erase, which therefore remained in her heart. Perhaps because of this past, she felt that no one had ever loved her. As a result, her marriage was not going well.

However, she came to realize that this experience was nothing other than her interior being reversed outward—that it was born of the unbroken pattern that had passed down through generations of her family through her grandmother and mother to herself. Her feelings toward her parents changed completely once she understood that they too sought happiness but had no control over it. Then the memories she had created based on her assumptions changed, and many long-forgotten happy memories of her father, such as playing on his lap, were resurrected. She, who had looked upon her childhood only with sadness, was now able to tell her childhood self that everything was all right.

Upon realizing that she actually was loved by her father, she felt liberated in her heart—and then she suddenly received a phone call from her father, whose whereabouts she had not known for decades. Their conversation flowed as if they had seen each other just the day before. All her past sufferings vanished when he uttered the words, "I have never forgotten about you, even for a day." Because the maleness in her interior was put back in order, it was inevitable that her relationship with her husband changed greatly as well.

Reports like this are innumerable. In one case, a child who experienced unbearable bullying was able to forget those horrible incidents as if all past data had been erased. Even if he did remember an incident, it was simply a painless memory and did not at all affect the him of the present.

So, what about the future? You cannot help but enjoy every moment of your life once you know the future is already here. You are in a space where everything has already been accomplished.

In chapter 2, which covers the trap of reversal, I discussed the fact that some people succeed but their unconsciousness surfaces and their success is reversed; however, there are those who succeed without experiencing reversal because they know they are already successful. There are also people who perceive naturally that time is flowing from the future. For them, there is no doubt about success; in their "I" of the present, they already possess information that enables them to succeed as well as the sensation they will have when they are successful. Nothing is more powerful than being aware that you are already accomplished and know the you of the future.

Before I met my partner, my life was a series of ups and downs—and in accordance with the system of the third-dimensional world, the higher the upswing, the lower the downswing. Whenever I reached my limit, with nothing more that I could do, it was always the I of the future that saved me. When you are driven into an extreme corner, your thought process stops operating, and time on the straight line of past and future also disappears. The you of the future, who has already become what you wish, calls out to the space, saying, "It's all right" or providing the inspiration you need to make a breakthrough.

"This is how I want to be" is not in the future. If you continue to envision how you want to be someday in the third-dimensional world, where the future is on the extended line of the present, you will never reach it, because you will keep postponing "someday."

How, then, would it be in High-Dimensional Space by Reversal with Anti-vector? You can imagine whatever you desire and know that everything has already been realized. This sense will, without fail, lead you in that direction and materialize your thoughts. This is related to how your brain functions. Your brain gathers whatever is necessary for the direction you are heading toward. It is as if everything that constitutes you unites as a cheering squad to support you.

One could say that, good or bad, our world is one in which each individual creates his or her own unique universe. It is as if everyone is living in the same singular universe, but in his or her unique world. We merely share the physical universe that is defined by our own five senses. In other words, your universe hangs on your perception, and the universe completely depends upon it.

What, then, do we perceive in the space called the Now? People often speak of future security. But since the future is already here, absolute security is already here as well. In the space where everything is already accomplished, you will never be betrayed as long as you don't betray yourself. This is true even if you take a dream to its maximum extent. You never need to feel reserved toward anyone.

Through partnerunity, each and every one of us, with his or her unique and individual universe, will be united for the first time, forming a new universe. Couples will encounter hitherto unexperienced zones of humanity in the greatest domain of creation. This is the world of emptiness that Buddhism refers to. It is the source of creation and contains everything. The world we have tried to attain through asceticism or meditation can in fact be experienced in reality within the space of our daily lives.

How dynamic the field of creation called High-Dimensional Space by Reversal with Anti-vector is! There has never been anything greater than this, no matter how hard you strain yourself to imagine.

What is the furthest entity from humans? It is the existence called God, which entails the quintessence of division. The God that I refer to here is not the singular God of monotheism but rather the concept of the Creator.

Without God, there would be no humans, and without humans, the concept of God would not exist. However, the two opposite polarities are two sides of the same coin. Humans and God are polarities of the same nature, and from the beginning, they have never separated themselves from each other.

Originally, the existence called "you" and the power of creation were both parts of God's creation. Instead of placing God far away from yourself, if you realize and experience yourself and God as two sides of the same coin, you (who exist as God's fractal) will be able to freely use the power you wish—that is, godlike creativity—for the first time.

This new time and space even dismantles the concept of your birth. When you perceive events with the vector from the future and understand that time flows from the future to the past, it is clear that you were born by choosing your parents. If this is the case, why did you choose them in particular? Isn't it because they were the most appropriate to help you fulfill the purpose of your birth?

The DNA of your parents, which has been handed down from the past, connects you with the distortions of your parents' thoughts—namely, unconsciousness and blind spots. These distortions are precisely the hurdles that you have chosen to experience yourself.

In the third-dimensional world, with its one-directional temporal axis that flows from past to future, these distortions produce a chain of recurring life patterns that unfold from generation to generation. But if you can instead see these distortions through the space called the Now—which is created by two vectors, past to future and future to past—they will dissolve instantly, and the chain will be broken.

You may wonder, "Why was I born into this sort of family? I wanted to be born into a richer family. It would have been wonderful to have such and such parents." But at the precise moment you realize that you have in fact chosen your parents and your point of view is completely turned around, you will experience a sensation you never expected.

Furthermore, you, who have come to know this and practice its application, will become the hero of your family, ending its negative cycle in the High-Dimensional Space by Reversal with

Anti-vector. In this time and space, where the future and the past exist simultaneously, you will be able to heal and bring peace to your ancestors and save the children of the future.

For more information on the concept presented in this chapter, see Rossco's *I Choose You, Mom and Dad!* (Sankosha, 2013).

Chapter 7

ESCAPING THE TRAPS: COMPLETE REGENERATION THROUGH A NEW VIEWPOINT

High-Dimensional Reality and the Directionality of Human Evolution

When one gains the viewpoint of High-Dimensional Space by Reversal with Anti-vector, miracles occur in an instant. But they do not stop with the person who experiences them; rather, they expand everywhere. Actually, they only look like miracles because they are seen from a third-dimensional viewpoint. In the high-dimensional domain, they are a reality that anyone can bring about.

Many people have experienced a new domain by escaping the traps that humans have fallen into. At the initial stage, I called these experiences miracles, because they happen in an extremely short period of time and are unimaginable according to conventional common sense. In truth, miracles have become a reality that anyone can readily bring about, now that many have begun to understand the system. By applying it, they have started to acquire the abilities to consciously alter phenomena.

Phenomena that are considered unbelievable according to the laws of nature in the third-dimensional domain are called miracles. But these same phenomena become natural in a space that has transcended the third-dimensional domain. Moreover, this reality is experienced not only by those who understand the system, but also by their family, friends, and others around them, sparking a chain reaction. This occurs because what you perceive in the space between you and another person is realized in your universe. Allow me to cite some reports that I've received.

A woman who was distressed about being sterile became pregnant soon after she came to understand herself through the system and gave birth to a healthy baby girl. Her friends and acquaintances who sought advice for their own sterility problems also became pregnant and gave birth, one after another. As soon as a father whose son had been socially withdrawn for many years came to understand that he was seeing in his son the reflection of himself, he was able to accept his son; the son subsequently came out of his room and soon returned to society.

Another woman was present when her uncle was told he had cancer. She even saw the X-ray showing the disease in focus. She decided to perceive that her uncle was well, and having secured peace of mind upon the harmonization of her marriage balance, she discovered at the next examination that his cancer had disappeared. A man who was helpless in the face of his parent's dementia came to understand his inner maleness, upon which the speech and behavior of his parent returned to normal. We hear countless examples such as these.

Note that understanding the system means applying and practicing it. It is not a study or accumulation of knowledge. You may feel you have understood it and say, "Okay, I've got the theory. That unpleasant husband is reflecting my interior, right." But if you keep saying, "I can't forgive that aspect of my husband" or "This is what I don't like about my husband," then nothing will change. If you truly understand that the reason you don't like your husband's speech and behavior is that it is a reflection of your interior, inner conflicts will disappear, and peace of mind will emerge. Moreover, you will see the results, in which phenomena change without fail before your eyes.

Once you are released from the past, you can experience the joy of creation to your heart's content. You will be astounded to discover that you can make any phenomenon, large or small, happen according to your desire. This will make you realize how much you have been constrained by the limitations of the third-dimensional world until now.

No matter how normal your life appears, there is a unique story in each and every person. The life that you have been treating as something indistinct in the third-dimensional world will start to stand out as your own unique drama.

When you see the structure of your life by using the system, with yourself as the origin of your universe, the intent behind the creation of such a life will gradually be revealed. For humans living in their own universe, the most riveting stories are their own, over and above those of any drama or movie. And once your story becomes clear, you can move the pieces on the chessboard of your life in any way you wish.

The Reality of Quantization of the Macro Domain

The reason your thoughts are materialized as reality is because you can control the world of quantum mechanics (the micro) from the position of Miross (the macro). As shown in figure 15, the act of seeing means that you, the micro, are looking at the expanse of space, called the macro—in short, the outer world.

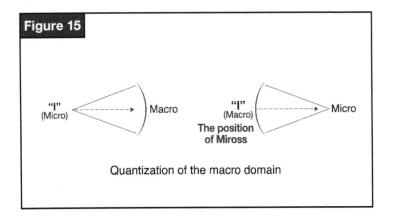

Quantization of the macro domain

What, then, is it like to look at the interior? It means trying to see the micro. But the world of quantum mechanics, the micro, does not reveal its true image when an observer of macro, called a body, comes into the picture. When an observer is involved, phenomena change. This is the dilemma of quantum physics. If you try to see the micro, you instantly become a point, meaning a micro yourself; the micro is then reversed to the macro, and you can no longer see the micro.

Let's consider this from a different angle. Suppose "I" try to see the source of my existence (figure 16). If our first ancestors were Adam and Eve, then space expands from them along the continuum of time, and humankind grows infinitely. However, if I try to observe Adam and Eve, I become a point, and Adam and Eve become a macro's expanse, even if I want to see the point as Adam and Eve.

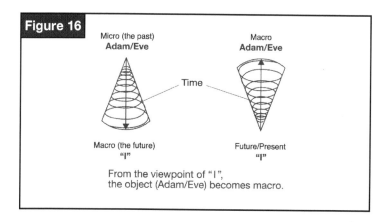

Figure 16

Micro (the past)
Adam/Eve

Macro
Adam/Eve

Time

Macro (the future)
"I"

Future/Present
"I"

From the viewpoint of "I",
the object (Adam/Eve) becomes macro.

By attaining the dimensionally displaced position of Miross, however, we are able to see the micro from the viewpoint of macro—in other words, I from the macro can see Adam and Eve, the micro. This means that I can overview everything with complete objectivity. I, being divided into two, experience conflicts as ego. The world as you truly desire will unfold through the quantization of the macro domain without the presence of ego as it materializes consciousness.

The Role of Miross in Changing the World

Amid various social problems, families and married couples are the pivotal point; society has struggled to reexamine this. Yet we may wonder what kind of families and marriage partners we should be.

Why do we so often hear tragic news, even about elite and wealthy families that are widely envied? Why are there so many divorces of supposedly ideal couples who seemed the very picture of happiness? Why do people despise their parents? Why do married couples continue to be contentious? The real solutions to the problems of families and individuals, which cannot be imagined from external appearances, cannot be attained in the third-dimensional system.

We hear phrases like "Take good care of your parents," "Married couples should maintain a loving relationship," and "Be considerate of others." Though these may appear to be obvious mottos, they all have meaning. Once you see the mechanism, you will understand clearly what parents, married couples, and other people really are. In a world where everything seems indistinct and poorly perceived, the essence is hidden. The human program, which has been groping along ineffectually amidst the superficial reality, is nearing its end.

Those who generate questions already know the answers. After all, the only answer that can truly convince you is the one you come up with yourself, because the world is none other than what you have created. Only by reaching the genuine answer yourself through the application of the system—not by relying on someone else or through prayer—can you enter the world in which you are able to resolve all your problems and never be faced with the same problem again. This is indeed the high-dimensional reality that anyone can experience.

In this book, I have written about the mechanism of human relationships. Perhaps we could think about it in the following way. Your relationships with others—including your family, friends, and people at work—generate various emotions. In turn, these emotions are manifested as different phenomena, one after another. What if this chain of relationships evolves to the level of creating social phenomena? Perhaps when we go that far, the relationships become so complicated that we no longer grasp the causation.

You may think that incidents occurring in society are no concern of yours. However, it is quite possible that your emotions, such as your sense of deficiency or anger, are the cause of events in society today. Although you may not think that these events have anything to do with you, it could be said that you bear part of the responsibility. If this is the case, by rewinding your life and erasing the sense of lack and anger in yourself, you may be able to sever the chain of reactions that has originated from you. If each and every one of us were to work on ourselves with this understanding, we would have the power to reverse social phenomena.

If we can use the system to end individual problems before they occur, with their aggregation, the world will surely change. This is because by accepting others as yourself, each and every one of us will be able to end his or her own inner battle and actively change all aspects of society in the world, as together, we constitute society. As I have said before, ending the battle in each and every person is not a farfetched idea. Once enough people begin to apply the system as a concrete technique, a sudden transformation will occur.

Countries currently in the midst of war or people beset by tragedy may not have enough space to even think about dismantling or dissecting themselves. That is why those who can do so now should do so first. I have communicated Miross with this in mind. Those with whom my thoughts have resonated and who have applied the system have surely changed and even started to introduce Miross to others around them.

People are involved in conflicts, fighting and killing each other. In spite of the teachings of the saints and extraordinary scientific discoveries and accomplishments, this aspect of human nature has not changed since the dawn of history. Rather, history has continually repeated itself, and our egos have grown exponentially—even to the point of devouring the earth that our very existence depends upon. We seem to have reached a watershed between survival and destruction.

Chapter 8

STORIES OF TRANSFORMATION

People Who Have Transcended the Human
Program and Embarked on a New Way of Living

*The change you experience through the application of Miross happens in an
instant. But it does not stop at the practitioner; it is also channeled to friends,
family members, coworkers, and others, one after another.*

I would like you to see the mechanisms of relationship
through accounts of people who have overcome various problems
by practicing the Miross system. Among the many examples we
have in different fields, I address phenomena that are seen as
social problems, including stalking, schizophrenia, and divorce.
These people have changed their lives by understanding the
mechanism of relationship.

How to Prevent Stalking

*In cases of stalking, the countdown to catastrophe begins when the two
people involved meet. In undoing the relationship between the victim and the*

offender based on the Miross system, you can see how an unthinkable process had already started to take shape below the surface.

As stalking incidents occur frequently, this relationship system is one I most certainly would like people to learn for prevention. Most cases of stalking are by so-called rejected suitors involved in a romantic relationship, and it is said that 90 percent of the victims are women. There is no end of reports from female victims who fear stalking behaviors by men they know from current or past relationships. It is important to know that these incidents result from people not understanding the relationship system and, for that reason, becoming entrapped.

This may be difficult for family members and others who are close to the victims to accept; however, by knowing the relationship system, you will be able to actualize a society that can secure your safety and that of your family while halting the creation of victims or offenders.

A man, Mr. B, was assigned to the department where a thirty-year-old woman, Ms. A, worked. One day, as they were leaving work, they began to converse, and the talk touched on private matters. She happened to mention her dissatisfaction with her marriage, and this triggered a sense of intimacy that led to their affair. As he was also married, the relationship was double adultery. Perhaps because it was a secretive love affair, the relationship quickly grew in intensity, even to the point that they promised to get divorced and marry each other.

But around the time Ms. A's divorce was finalized, their relationship started to break down. Mr. B, who had until then been kind and gentlemanly, suddenly became domineering and tried to control her with his demands. At first, she tried hard to meet his expectations, even though his demands were unreasonable, because she had already grown extremely dependent on him and felt she could not live without him. Her dissatisfaction increased, however, as she tried to accommodate him. Although she had perceived him as an ideal man, his faults became increasingly conspicuous.

Ms. A's feelings for him diminished rapidly as she started noticing his abnormal nature, such as his egocentric behavior and extreme attachments to things as well as aggressiveness and implacability toward others when things did not go well. Mr. B, meanwhile, felt bewildered by this drastic change in Ms. A, who had been devoted to him. He became obsessed with the delusion that she might have found someone else, and his anger toward her started to mount as he realized he could no longer control her.

At last, she broached the subject of separating. This caused an immediate, drastic escalation in his behavior. He held her in captivity, freeing her only after he had forced her—at knifepoint and under threat of death—to promise that she would do anything he demanded of her for the rest of her life. Even after this, she continued to receive dozens of phone calls from him each day. Even worse, the man started to involve people around her, and they too started receiving slanderous calls about her.

Mr. B's calls indicated that he was monitoring Ms. A's every move. Frightened that she was being kept under constant surveillance, she could not even leave her house. It got to the point where she would have a panic attack if she so much as saw reports of similar cases on television. Driven to the breaking point, she summoned the courage to contact the police, who issued a strict injunction against Mr. B, thanks to Ms. A's record of his calls and the report she had filed following her confinement. Finally, the stalking stopped.

Fortunately, this situation did not develop into a major incident like some cases in the news. However, even though her relationship with him had ended, she could not rest easy—for Mr. B was not the cause of the stalking incident. The relationship unfolded as it did due to Ms. A's inner unconscious emotions, which allowed her to attract such a partner and enter into this disastrous relationship.

There is a pattern in relationships that explains how two people with the same emotional sentiments are attracted to each other based on their experiences. Ever since her childhood, Ms. A had been unable to feel the love of her parents. From the way they treated her, she had assumed that she was not loved. Because of that assumption, she continually picked up the feeling that she was not loved or accepted by anyone. As a result, she constantly undervalued her own existence.

Feeling that there was no longer joy in her life, Ms. A sought the sensation of being genuinely alive. She began trying to act as others wished in order to gain love and acceptance from those she loved. However, trying to act as others wished meant being controlled by them. Gradually, she began to feel confined; as a result, she fell into a pattern of ending relationships abruptly. This became the pattern of her human relationships.

Ms. A later practiced the Miross system, and in the process of dissecting herself, she came to understand the situation clearly.

If she had remained as she was, she would have again, through her same unconsciousness, attracted the same type of man and entered into an unwanted relationship. She therefore feels genuinely relieved to know the system.

Mr. B, on the other hand, who grew up in a wealthy family, experienced his parents' divorce when he was a child and grew up craving love and affection from them. He thought of himself as a nuisance and unwanted child, for he was often scolded and punished in the name of discipline. Like Ms. A, he sensed that he was unloved. As a result, he was filled with anger and desire for revenge.

He too was searching for people who accepted him. When he found a woman who could, he acted like a gentleman and demonstrated other behaviors his partner wanted to see—at the beginning. Soon his aggressive character appeared, though, and he dared his partner, saying, "I've acted the way you wanted me to. Now you have to do as I say." He would try to take total control of his partner. He too fell into the same pattern in his relationships.

Around the time the two met, Ms. A had already been looking for someone new who could truly understand her, because she felt that she and her husband did not share the same values. As for Mr. B, he had been looking for a place for himself, as he could not feel his worth at home or work. Without realizing that their neediness drew them together, the two felt attracted to each other and ended up becoming partners.

Both of them possessed a great sense of deficiency or lack and felt extreme joy when they were able to fulfill themselves by being together. For this reason, they were able to maintain a wonderful relationship at first. However, the sense of deficiency or lack, born of their assumptions, that had attracted them to each other created the mere illusion of being ideal partners. As a result, the relationship was extremely fragile and could start to unravel at any moment. This mechanism of relationship is germane not only to the phenomenon of stalking, but also to ordinary married couples.

Looking back, Ms. A reflects, "Even though I was terrified about being under constant surveillance, it was my extreme sense of lacking, the wanting of my partner to only focus on me and to be with me all the time, that became reversed and materialized as such a phenomenon. I never imagined that it was a phenomenon that I created myself."

This was a couple in which both parties had the same qualities, but one blamed herself and shut herself off while the other attacked his partner because she did not accept him. Only their ways of expressing themselves were different: between a self-torturing person (Ms. A) and an assaultive person (Mr. B), the relationship of victim and offender was established. However, when seen from a different point of view, it was a tragedy that occurred because they had fallen into traps without knowing the system of relationships.

The number of stalking cases continues to grow, but the ones reported on television are only those that have developed into serious crimes; actually, similar cases occur more frequently around you. Though people today are more conscious of crime prevention and self-protection, it is important for each and every one of us to understand the relationship system to prevent tragic incidents.

When something happens in a relationship, you need to understand the reason by observing yourself from a high-dimensional domain based on the relationship system before you complicate the situation by becoming overwhelmed with fear. If you can do this, the situation will surely change for the better. This is the surest way to protect yourself and your family and to eventually eradicate such sad incidents from the world.

When Schizophrenia Strikes

When it comes to mental illness, we often hear about schizophrenia and depression. The symptoms vary, but hallucinations and delusions are typical, and it can become difficult to maintain a normal lifestyle. This in turn creates mental stress and confusion, not only for the person afflicted, but also for the family. The following example describes the process of regeneration that took place very rapidly between a daughter who experienced a drastic change and her family.

The oldest daughter of Ms. T had been married for one year and was in a wonderful relationship with her husband. She seemed to enjoy both work and her hobbies to the fullest extent. However, she suddenly said that she felt scared and could no longer go to work. Soon she became unable to perform even household work and began having auditory hallucinations. Her behavior escalated to an extreme that included crying, shouting, strangling her husband, and even trying to jump off the balcony.

"I already knew about Miross," said Ms. T, "but when I saw my daughter completely broken down, I was so confused that I just couldn't do anything during the first week. My son-in-law, my husband (who is my daughter's stepfather), and I were seriously trying to grasp what was happening."

In fact, when her daughter was three years old, Ms. T herself had been admitted to the psychiatric department of a hospital due to mental instability. Her condition was the result of trying to raise a child in a totally new environment as well as her fixation on being perfect and performing the role of a good wife and wise mother. Despite her efforts, her first marriage later ended in divorce.

"In my fifty years of life," she said, "no matter what the experience, I kept telling myself that everything was fine. Even when I had a mental breakdown, I thought I had overcome it by falling back on the positive thinking taught by a certain religion I practiced. Later, I began to work in healing and counseling. Because I had healed many desperate people who were full of anxieties, I had never felt scared, nor was I aware that there was, in fact, a bottomless fear within me."

Soon after birth, Ms. T was sent to her relatives as an adopted child; however, she was returned to her family, which consisted of her parents and siblings, when she was ten years old. The feelings of isolation and confusion when she was reunited with her family, suffering she underwent in her first marriage and raising her children single-handedly after her divorce, and ill heath after starting to work—all these emotions of fear and anxiety had been kept sealed within her.

"I was afraid of facing the fear itself, which I had always concealed," she said. "But one day, when I finally said, 'I'm scared,' my current husband closed his eyes, looked inside himself, and soon cried out that he also had fear within him. I felt as though the fear in me was sucked into my husband and vanished. He then shared the various fears that had been locked inside of him for sixty years. We also shared the sensations of guilt that we felt when we heard our daughter say, 'I'm sorry,' coupled with 'I'm scared.'

"We were not in contact with my daughter for two weeks after her symptoms began, but we continued to observe intensely the fear and sense of guilt that she had thrust upon us—because what she demonstrated to us was simply our own selves. And during those two weeks, she nearly became able to lead a normal life."

How did her daughter's husband deal with the situation at the time? Ms. T said, "My husband asked my daughter's husband what he saw of himself in his wife, if it was something he unconsciously hid from himself. His response was that she wanted to be liberated; this was also the way he felt about himself. He understood that, and as soon as he did, he burst into laughter, saying it was like a comedy and that he no longer feared anything.

"He went on to take care of her, at times not even sleeping, and said he would be fine even if she was like this for five or ten years. He even took her to work by making a special request to the president of his company. My husband said with admiration, 'Although as an architect, he has his own office, bringing his wife, with her strange behavior, including talking to herself and crying, is quite extraordinary for a typical man in our society.' When I was hospitalized during my previous marriage, my first husband was absolutely indifferent. My daughter's husband showed the kind of love from a man that I most wanted to feel. I truly felt healed."

Three weeks after her daughter's symptoms had first appeared, Ms. T received an e-mail while conducting a seminar in another region. Her daughter's message read, "Mom, how was your seminar? You know what? I was able to prepare lunch for my husband today!" From that point on, her daughter recovered and was able to focus on her household chores and began enjoying her hobbies. Six months later, she found a job that was perfect for her and so returned to society. It was as if she had been reborn in a form more like herself. Ms. T and her husband were also liberated from the oppression they had kept hidden within themselves for so long. Relaxed, they began enjoying the new path that had opened to them.

There is even a sequel to the story. Ms. T's ex-husband passed away, and she and her daughters received a huge inheritance. "I was really surprised, as I didn't even know that he had passed away," she said. Ms. T found out that in her ex-husband's family, there had been a long line of mental disorders. Her ex-husband had been bipolar, and he had feared and hated his bloodline.

"My daughter, who had inherited the bloodline from my ex-husband and me, was able to end what had been passed on from generation to generation by making it take form as a phenomenon. I believe that this inheritance was a gift of thanks from my ex-husband as well as my ancestors."

Reviving a Dead Marriage

It was a marriage that had been fervently sought, as the couple loved each other very much, but they became the worst of enemies. Nevertheless, they were somehow able to avoid a divorce and continue living together, though only by ignoring each other. But even a married couple such as this, whose relationship was practically dead, was able to restore their love. The wife's determination is what revived this family on the verge of collapse.

From the outside, Mr. and Mrs. H and their two daughters, one in elementary school and the other in middle school, looked like the ideal family. However, the relationship between the couple was reaching its lowest point. They had gotten married because they had loved each other deeply. However, their relationship had cooled to the point of collapse, although they did not even know how this had happened, as there was no particular reason.

"We hated each other," said Mrs. H. "My husband would say he wanted to rent another house or that he wanted to live separately in the same house, remodeling it so we could leave each other alone and do whatever we liked, only to live this way for the sake of the children. He even showed me a house remodeling plan. After seventeen years of marriage as husband and wife, I still did not understand him at all. The closest yet the farthest existence in the world to me—that was my husband."

How had this happened? The cause was concealed in Mrs. H's personal background, as well as assumptions about herself. "When my mother was twenty years old," said Mrs. H, "she became pregnant with me; her marriage to my father was due to this unintended pregnancy. My father didn't really work, so my mother worked day and night and even faced domestic violence at his hands. When I was in sixth grade, my mother asked me if it was okay with me if she got divorced. I loved her very much and only wanted her to be happy, so I responded yes. I dreamed about living with her and my brother, the three of us together. But instead, my mother left with my brother, telling me that I'd be fine staying with my father because I was mature enough. I felt absolutely abandoned."

Her mother subsequently took her back, but from that point, sad experiences began to occur again. "My mother changed partners one after another. Despite the way she was, I still loved her very much and wanted to continue living with her. But she kept saying she wanted to be happy as a woman, rather than as a mother, and that she would never have married my father if I hadn't been born. Because of this, I've lived with a constant sense of guilt for coming into the world. I told myself over and over that I wasn't necessary for my mother's happiness and I wasn't worthy of being loved."

Despite these experiences, Mrs. H did find someone to love, got married, and was blessed with a lovely child. However, contrary to her wishes, she ended up following in her mother's footsteps. "My mother always suffered from her relationships with her partners. Even though she changed partners often, she could never find happiness. One day, I realized that if I continued to live this way, I would end up creating the same situation for my daughters, too. I felt emphatically that I did not give birth to my daughters to let them live like this. It was after I had felt this from the very bottom of my heart that I came to learn about Miross."

Mrs. H started practicing Miross with an iron determination to revive her family no matter what. She went on to discover herself by understanding the mechanism that had created the situation she found herself in. If she felt that she was not worthy of being loved, how could she expect her partner or anyone else to love her? It seemed she had rejected love or bounced it back, saying she could not accept or believe it—all the while actually craving and longing for love. Since her husband had also been drawn to her because of the same wounds he carried within himself, what she threw back distanced him further.

"To go on to discover myself was an amazing thing," she said. "Once I came to understand the mechanism that had locked me inside of my own unconsciousness, I was able to feel my true self, which I had never been aware of. I was determined to rebirth myself by putting myself back into my womb along with my daughters and husband. Then I understood that the true nature of his anger was loneliness, resulting from my ignorance toward him. I, who had never understood love, was just running after my own loneliness, and I had never really seen him. The loneliness of his childhood and that of my childhood were of the same magnitude. I became aware that when he shouted, 'Goddamn it!' to me, he was actually crying out and saying, 'Please love me; please accept me.' This was the same voice that I had suppressed within myself."

It was inevitable that these thoughts would be transmitted to her husband. Soon he too began to practice the system in earnest, and their marital and family situation changed drastically. Mrs. H said, "I think that when I changed my attitude from 'I want to change my partner' to 'You're fine as you are'—and I truly felt that way—the relationship started to change. 'You're fine as you are' were the words I had always wished to hear. That's why my husband was making it so difficult for me to accept him and kept shouting, 'How could you love a horrible man like me?' I couldn't help but think that our ancestors too suffered in the same situation.

"We had kept on denying ourselves and didn't know how to go about communicating with each other. However, we have been able to laughingly put an end to many things in the space we have created between us, saying the magic phrase, 'Oh, *that's* how it is!' We both have become aware of the fact that we loved each other very much and were in fact of immeasurable value to each other." The change in the two went on to affect not only their daughters, but also the husband's relatives as well as Mrs. H's mother.

"Once we became happy, everyone became happy," said Mrs. H. "I realized that my mother and I were just repeating the same pattern. Our desire for happiness, which we sought earnestly, had simply gotten reversed. I hadn't known that regardless of what happens to me, if I simply understand, 'Oh, *that's* how it is' based on the Miross system, we could be happy. My mother hadn't known that either, and I now understand that she was simply the way she had to be. Now I have a mother who always supports me and sincerely rejoices in the fact that I've become happy. I was able to accept my past as I got to know Miross and understand that I actually set up my life this way in order to have the best experience possible as a human being. Now, together with my husband, I'm able to change the bitter past and create the future. I am happy simply as I am."

What I have introduced here are all difficult and traumatic experiences. You may think that you are just an ordinary person who has never had such traumatic experiences, and therefore, they have nothing to do with you. However, you may notice that there is a certain pattern in these relationships. No pattern is either big or small: its seed always lurks in seemingly ordinary, trivial misunderstandings between husband and wife or conflicts between parents and children. Even people who are considered fortunate, who have no particular problems and didn't grow up in a miserable family environment, are the same. They too have conflicts inside.

Whether or not you recognize what you are experiencing as conflict, as long as you live in the conventional human program, you won't feel fulfilled. If, on the other hand, you know the pattern of a relationship, you will be able to get through any hardship, no matter what happens, and stand tall in a new sphere. It will be possible for you to live in peace. Let me introduce a final example.

The Partnerunity of a Couple

The truth, unimaginable from conventional concepts, has been concealed between a man and a woman. Creation by the two through their partnerunity inspires the ultimate experience of self-realization, which could never have occurred if created by one. What did this couple see when they returned to being one consciousness after having achieved balance in their interior?

The man, sickly since birth, wandered between life and death until he reached adulthood. Among the variety of symptoms he suffered, asthma in particular made him feel close to death. However, between the difficult breaths of an asthma attack, he often had a sense of being able to observe his body from above. Thereafter, he gained the power to see through the ambiguity of third-dimensional reality.

Unbound by any social restraints, he repeatedly experienced extraordinary success in his work. However, when success swings to its polarity, an equal degree of failure simultaneously exists at the other polarity. Severe blows tormented him for a long time. Still, from the bottom of his heart, he held on to a conviction that he would someday obtain something super-extraordinary. No matter what happened, that conviction never wavered.

The woman, after having an experience that almost overturned her life, was searching for a pillar, a reason to live. Grasping at straws, she waited for the time to come. She felt from the bottom of her heart that she had a role to play in influencing the transformation of the consciousness of human beings.

In 1999, an inevitable process drew this man and woman together. The man sensed an intellect in her that he had never before encountered. The woman felt infinite human potential in him. The two discovered afterward that these were feelings they had possessed all along, and they understood that as a pair, they were the perfect combination. At the same time, they came to know their roles and futures.

They therefore knew what they had to do: superimpose the system of the universe on the dimension of the living man and woman and then apply this to daily life. The couple began with the process of knowing their selves and then equalizing the two opposite polarities. It brought about a series of never-before-experienced joys and pain at the same time, but they were able to succeed in bringing forth a system and methods for its practical application.

High-Dimensional Space by Reversal with Anti-vector of man and woman is the space of creation, transcending the third-dimensional domain. In this space, the two were able to achieve a union of infinite human potential and sublime intellect and discover the ultimate self-realization. Everything that each of them had hoped for was there. If practiced by only one of them, this system would have ended up as an unfinished dream, despite whatever experience or power he or she had. This example is the story of my partner and me, and the system called Miross had its birth here.

A f t e r w o r d

What I have conveyed in this book is not an account of a dream. It is a step toward the evolution of humankind, which has already begun.

My partner, Midori, and I have discovered an amazing world through our experiences together. The life before the two of us met and the life after have some connection, but they have become completely different lives.

Everyone has his or her own role in life. Our role was to dismantle the system of this world and show how to reconstruct it using ourselves, as man and woman, as the experimental subjects. This system isn't something we thought of; rather, it had already been prepared for us, to allow us to discover the way leading to evolution. We have waited a long time for this moment, and it is for this moment that lives have been passed from generation to generation.

Human problems are all born out of unfulfilled inner feelings, such as a sense of what is lacking or missing. Where do these feelings come from? Isn't it true that we feel this way because we already know the sense of fulfillment? If we have never felt fulfilled, how can we sense that something is lacking? Humans cannot recognize that something is lacking if there was nothing to start with. If this is so, then there is already something fulfilled in everyone.

Miross is not a technique to find a wound and heal it. Any incident, if observed from the viewpoint of Miross, can allow you to remove yourself from emotions and find certain patterns in your life. In this world, wounds just disappear through practicing the system.

You will discover an already fulfilled you inside yourself. You do not need to rely on anyone, because this is something anyone can do by himself or herself. Please take a look at the grand design of the high-dimensional symmetrical system found in chapter 3. Do you know that you are protected by the perfection of the system? You are already an inhabitant in the world of harmony.

When you understand the traps and can grasp High-Dimensional Space by Reversal with Anti-vector, you will be able to fulfill any dreams you wish in your universe of great harmony.

Being able to do as you wish may be understood to mean that someone else is being hurt or losing something according to third-dimensional thought. However, you need not worry, as there are no "others" in the high-dimensional domain.

To know yourself is to know the world and the universe. At the moment of death, we humans may be able to overview our lives in a split second from a high-dimensional position. If this is so, then why can't we overview our lives from a high-dimensional position while we are still alive? Even if the lives that we have walked through so far have been miserable, we should never give up. Everything you have experienced so far was fine in itself.

You now stand on a hill from which you can overview the incidents of the past, things about your parents, your children, and your ancestral roots, as well as your future. So let us take a step forward toward a new life without any fear or worries. Live as *arugamama*, the way you are. All of your dreams have already been realized.

About the Author

Rossco is the founder and president of Miross Institute and the creator of Miross, a revolutionary new thought system developed through thirty years of research. Together with his wife, Midori, he is dedicated to introducing Miross to the world as the ultimate measure of conscious evolution with the capacity to eliminate all problems and create a society of absolute peace. He and his wife live in Kobe, Japan.

For more information about Rossco and Miross, visit <u>www.rossco.jp</u>.

Made in the USA
Middletown, DE
30 August 2021